412 Monroe

Stephen Crimaudo

412 Monroe

Stephen Crimaudo

ISBN 978-1-304-04353-5

Chapter 1: The Apartment and the Crew

"Jimmy, where's my wallet?!" Johnny bellowed to his younger brother as we all turned, half asleep and maybe still half drunk to watch the show.

"How the hell should I know?" barked Jimmy in reply.

It was almost 10:00 am on a Saturday morning after a classic all night bender in Hoboken, N.J. A good crew assembled in the old apartment on Friday night for the festivities.

The roommates were Johnny and Jimmy McCauley who lived in the once grand apartment with Mark O'Dell, or Odie as he was known to everyone. Odie was a long-time family friend of the McCauley's from back in the early days in Wellesley, Massachusetts.

Rounding out the entourage were Jude Brautigan and Danny Afflitto, who went to St. Joseph's University in Philadelphia with Jude and Johnny. Jude and Danny somehow managed to remain sleeping through the increasingly louder exchange between the two McCauleys. Jude was always a solid sleeper. Danny was always a little more focused and determined and as a result landed a serious job as a trader on Wall Street with Cantor Fitzgerald.

"Jimmy, I know you had it last night!" Johnny yelled to the now awakening collection of semi-comatose bodies.

In random positions throughout the apartment were Rich Schleifer and Jeff Snyder, who made the trip up from Brick Township on Friday night and were initially connected to the group, as I was, through Jude. Jeff, always referred to as Heffe, was a product of the central Jersey shore town of Brick and was a reliable source of entertaining hook up stories. Heffe also owned and skillfully operated a nice sized open bow, center console fishing boat. Many summer weekends were spent down at Heffe's house in Brick drinking and fishing and hitting the shore bars.

John and Jimmy McCauley, Mark O'Dell and Jude Brautigan compromised the young, successful and good looking (and overly confident because of those facts) second and third generation Irish boys with whom I had decided to spend most of my free time.

During the winter months of 1993 hard driving music from bands like Pearl Jam, Stone Temple Pilots and Nirvana dominated the airwaves of the New York rock stations and the local music scene. Bill Clinton was in his first term as President and *Jurassic Park* was the top grossing film. I had finally graduated from Rutgers University in May and landed a job in nearby Jersey City for an environmental consulting firm managing the assessment of contaminated sites that were the by-product of that city's industrial past.

We were all relatively young, in our mid to late twenties, recently graduated from college and single. And on any given weekend we would make the short migration up from the central Jersey towns of Old Bridge, South River and East Brunswick to Hoboken and the old railroad apartment on Monroe Street.

The destination at 412 Monroe Street was a nearly one-hundred-year-old, six story walk up brownstone in a marginal Italian and Spanish neighborhood.

Due to its proximity to the relatively bad and mostly Latino projects two blocks west, the landlord kept the building locked up tighter than Fort Knox. The required tight security caused anyone who wanted access to the apartment to conduct a complicated series of phone calls from the corner deli (since this was the era before cell phones) and shouts to and from the bedroom window just to get in through front door. Eventually, and after much trial and error, an ingenious system was developed to speed up the process which involved a quick phone call from the deli and a toss of the keys from the bedroom window.

One late night after I tried in vain to wake up the boys by calling, I finally resorted to banging on the outside door. My pounding managed to really tick off the owner of the building who greeted me with a loaded 9mm Beretta handgun, and since I was a former Marine, the handgun didn't rattle me that much. So, after telling him not to point a loaded weapon at me I explained that I was staying with my friends upstairs and he finally let me in.

Once through the outer barrier of the front door you could finally stand in the foyer and wait for the buzzer to pass through the inner door and walk into the inside stairwell. A quick bound up a few flights of stairs and you were in the palace that was the hub for our strategy and planning for the evening's festivities and the arena for the incessant intellectual boxing match that inevitably sprang up, in my case as soon as I walked into the front door.

Jab! "Crimapaldi (my actual name would elude these boys for almost another year) what's up with that haircut?" said Johnny.

No one was spared. Once, upon noticing that I was wearing my shiny, new running sneakers for our night out (a tactical error, I admit) Johnny bellowed, loud enough for everyone in the apartment to hear, "Dude, I didn't know you were wearing the show stoppers!"

When Odie would break out his stylish, but possibly formal vest, Johnny would, without fail, break out into the chorus from Kenny Roger's, *the Gambler,*

"*...you got to know when to hold 'em,*

know when to fold 'em..."

All of this came from a guy who constantly and proudly wore a T-shirt, as a zinger to then president Clinton, stating: "Smoke Dope; Dodge the Draft, Cheat on Your Wife; Become President: The American Dream", on the front, and "Vote GOP" on the back.

The boxing match continued.

Uppercut! "Dude, that shirt is going to hurt you. I guarantee you don't get any tale in that thing," followed Jude.

I typically smiled and took the heat, knowing that it was all in good fun and everyone would have their turn stepping into the spotlight.

Jude came from a strong and devout Catholic family and was as quick to help you, as he did for me often, as he would zing you if you deserved it. He was a fare haired and blue-eyed Irishman who constantly made everyone aware of the *German Hammer.*

Some of the other characters were better at lobbing a quick grenade at the other targets in the room, like Danny, who had the ability to take a quick measure of a potential competitor and make an early and devastating hit. Others, like me for example, were simply easy targets.

"Jimmy! I'm not kidding, what did you do with my wallet and my keys?" Jonny yelled. The performance continued with the now wide awake group of spectators waiting for Jimmy's quick witted reply.

"Johnny, you are such a complete jackass that you probably left it in the cab we took home!" The laughter from the audience signaled the approval of the show and the beginning of a fun Saturday morning in the apartment.

The two McCauley brothers were fun to watch. Since they were cut from the same Irish cloth as Odie and Jude, Jimmy and Johnny were great to have on your side and to be around. Jimmy was quick witted and innately funny, tall and square jawed like all the four brothers in the family, and physically tough. (For a while I referred to Jimmy as a "young Kirk Douglas." It was possibly a stretch, but it was close enough.) Johnny was a bit thinner than Jimmy at the time and slightly taller, as the tale of the pre-fight weigh in would record it, and much more talkative. Johnny, or J Mac, was also naturally funny, and when the two were together the laughs were nonstop.

"Let's look for the keys after we eat" I said in a fruitless effort to change the subject and really to get something to eat.

The layout of 412 Monroe Street was a hybrid of a classic railroad apartment and an older brownstone walk up. A left turn upon entering through the front door led you into the kitchen with the ancient Amana *RadarRange* microwave oven that the McCauley brothers permanently borrowed from their parent's garage. Past the kitchen was a huge dining room which was adjacent to the equally large den and living room. Around a right-hand corner was a center bedroom that you needed to walk through to finally get to the two back bedrooms and a second bathroom. A right turn at the front door allowed you to bypass the splendor that was the living and dining rooms and take the long hallway to the bathroom and back bedrooms. The apartment was large, solid and built to last, a perfect setting for the weekend trips to Hoboken.

The group was now wide awake and feeling the pain from Friday night's hard corps drinking. For the most part the drink of choice was pints of beer, any beer as long as it was good enough and cheap enough to drink all night long. Occasionally we ventured into the unknown and treacherous territory of hard liquor but we all eventually learned that with your old flame, pints of beer, your body could only absorb the alcohol as fast as you could physically drink the sixteen ounces in the pint. It was the perfect alchemy for the near alcoholic.

We were all weekend drunks, damn right, but we were the walking drunks and the functioning drunks (except, of course, when we weren't). On a typical Saturday morning the partying would eventually begin, and another piece of the puzzle would fall into place. The hangover would need relief and it's only a continuation of the same good, harmless fun. Once we were again feeling no pain, the silent bell announcing the next round was rung and, like the suddenly aware hound that smells his prey, we were all ready to pounce.

Odie started with a good zinger.

"Crimapaldi, did you hook up with that girl at Texas-Arizona (the name of a good bar, one of our favorites and spoken as one word) or was it another near miss?"

Odie had a healthy confidence level. He played soccer in High School and tried to stay in decent condition. Odie would somehow manage to fit in running and working out during the mid week when the rest of us weren't in the apartment drinking.

The *near miss* line generated a good laugh. I smiled in response because the phrase was mine, it belonged to me, it defined me, and I gladly accepted all of the implications. The *near miss* was the time spent talking to a girl, a close call, close enough to cause some impact but not enough to close the deal. I racked up many over the weeks and months of hanging out in Hoboken. It meant that I was always up at bat and always swinging, striking out sometimes though, but that wasn't the entire point. I knew that eventually a solid connection would occur, and I would soon hit the ball out of the park.

A futile attempt was made to make some recollection of the previous night. Who hooked up and who didn't, who thinks they have the potential to hook up tonight. We all trash talked and laughed and partied and trash talked some more. The stories kept coming, sparking the nearly dormant, faded and almost lost memories back to life.

"Oh, yea, I remember those girls, they dug me." or "Wasn't that after we left Texas Arizona?" or "What was the band that was playing at that other bar?" or "What time did we get back?" or "Where the fuck did Johnny disappear to?"

Jimmy usually had a great answer that went something like: "I don't remember a goddamn thing."

The memories are jolted to life, with some details coming into focus. Typically, there were always more questions than answers. It was a by-product of the constant haze of the drinking and partying, the cloud we're all in, the cause of the complete disappearance of inhibition and one of the main reasons we all had so much damn fun.

Now, if we collected six to eight friends and hung out in a huge old apartment all weekend and went out in northern New Jersey's version of Sin City, as Hoboken had become, we would still have a blast. There is no doubt about it, and the uninitiated may question the need for the added chemistry. But, if you take the same group of friends and throw them into the same apartment while adding a witch's brew of booze and partying, then you can light the fuse and watch the fun while we all blast off.

Chapter 2: The Comfortable Couch

A great way to pass the time in the apartment was to tell the stories generated from the fun of weekends past.

One story that was a consistent crowd pleaser on any given Saturday morning involved a *near miss* and the large sectional couch that anchored the den.

Before I started hanging out with the McCauleys, Jude, Odie and Danny at 412 Monroe on a recurring basis, I had an old and stiff, brown and gray plaid, basically ugly and large couch that I didn't need any longer. The couch was fairly comfortable and if your standards for décor were low enough (as they were for three, just out of college, Irishman who didn't have enough seating in their apartment) then this old, plaid couch was the perfect addition.

One weekday afternoon I dropped the couch off while Jimmy was home. Jimmy and I moved the large and heavy couch off my rented van and up the stairs and set it up in the den. After our demanding and admirable feat was accomplished, we decided to get pretty lit up to celebrate while hanging out on the *new* couch. From that point on the couch was usually referred to as the *comfortable couch* because

I was always trying to sell it as such, and because it really was pretty comfortable.

That couch served the apartment well for at least a full year while it took the abuse of spilled food and beer, always welcoming a weary and drunken man at any hour of the day or night. The couch was quite loyal and faithful, for a couch.

After a full year working in Jersey City and hanging in Hoboken my life changed a bit. My company offered the local project staff an opportunity to work overseas on a Defense Department project where we would do site assessment work on Anderson Air Force Base. Anderson happened to be on the western Pacific Island territory of Guam in the Marianas Islands. It was a chance to travel and get out of the Jersey City project office, so of course I jumped at it. It meant that I would be out of the Hoboken scene for a little while, but I planned on returning and when that happened, I would have all the momentum and energy from my overseas trip to add to the scene.

While I was gone I missed the boys and the partying, and to this day the formula that I use to manage the difference in time zones between the East Coast and the island territory of Guam is: If you call your friends when it is noon on Saturday in the Marianas Islands, it will be 10:00 pm on Friday night in Hoboken and your friends will be drinking.

After four months of working, scuba diving and some decent island partying I returned to New Jersey, via Honolulu and Waikiki Beach, Hawaii. The first weekend back we all went to Jude's brother Bernie's wedding. The very next weekend I drove up to a reunion and the usual great scene in Hoboken.

The one noticeable difference was that included among all the guys hanging out in the apartment were a couple of girls. The presence of the girls in the male dominated environment didn't slow down the drinking and partying though. That night we all drank, and trash talked while I told a few bad jokes that I picked up on my trip. After a little while we all left the apartment to hit scene and the great bars including Texas Arizona.

At maybe 2:00 am that night I made my way back to the apartment to find a couple of mules already asleep, including Jimmy in his room next to the den. To my surprise and for some unknown reason, one of the girls who was hanging out in the apartment earlier was now awake and in the den. (I would learn later that Odie was responsible for that fact.) Since I was fairly buzzed and always up for stepping up at bat to take a swing, I asked this girl to sit down next to me.

My line went something like “Why don't you sit down over here, it's a comfortable couch.”

What I didn't realize at the time was that while I was up at bat swinging wildly with my *comfortable couch* line creating another *near miss*, Jimmy was wide awake the whole time listening in on my terrible line and the non-action it produced. He was the fly on the wall that I didn't hear buzzing.

From that moment on, beginning the very next morning when Jimmy told the story, I was constantly reminded of my terrible and useless *comfortable couch* line. The story was repeated probably ten thousand more times over the next few months and eventually years.

Chapter 3: Competitive Sports

As time passed during the morning and after a few good stories, someone would usually break out a beat up old deck of cards and start a good game of *Asshole.* This was the corrupted, combat style of old school Bridge that occupied the time while we drank and partied and continued the absolutely thorough but good natured trash talking.

"Jimmy, honestly, where the hell are my keys and wallet? Johnny asked while we played and as a result of a sparked to life memory of his still unaccounted for keys and wallet.

"Johnny, would you please shut the fuck up about your goddamn wallet and keys." Jimmy snapped back the way any younger brother with the upper hand would while generating more laughter from the crowd.

It was early Saturday afternoon now and we were still in the apartment, we were hitting our stride and putting away the bottles of Budweiser at a pretty good clip. The empty cases would get stacked against the wall and the never-ending contest would begin.

"Ro Sham Bo!" Someone usually Johnny or Jimmy would announce. This was our code speak for Paper, Rock, Scissors and everyone was always in. This was how any and all of the dirty or boring chores were assigned: How the cases of empties were thrown out; how more cold cases of beer were bought and sometimes how large bar tabs were paid for. Nothing was volunteered for or decided simply, that would be far too easy and civilized.

We all formed a circle while sitting around the table in the combination den and living room. The hands would be raised, and the individual strategies would be weighed and decided while usually remaining unspoken. Sometimes, in an effort to psyche out your foe someone would inevitably blurt out how *rock* always wins, how *rock* is the toughest. With a large group of drunken and buzzed guys who were, by this time of the day, running on an intellectually bone-dry tank, just getting started was a challenge, more than a challenge it was nearly impossible.

"Rhhooo..." the hands would all unsteadily go up. One drunken fool would always commit an error, a false start, he would throw down his hand prematurely and the process would begin again.

"Rhooooo...Sham...Bo! Finally, we had a clean start while all the hands would enter the circle at nearly the same time (after all it wasn't the goddamn Olympics) and the judging would begin. All rocks, what a bunch of idiots. Now into our groove the competition would pick up steam.

"Ro Sham Bo!" A few papers a few rocks and a one scissor.

"Shit!" Finally, a clean throw, all rocks and one paper! We had a clear winner and a chance for one lucky mule to exit out, have another victory beer and watch the action from a comfortable and safe distance off the front lines. Finally, only two are left and the throwing is fast and intense.

"Ro Sham Bo!" Two papers... again two papers... two scissors. The strategy is coming to the surface. Finally, one paper and one rock!

"Shit! Goddamn rock sucks!" The looser had to honor his commitment and take out the now huge stack of empty cases of beer. Tough break we all thought to ourselves, damn glad it was the other unlucky bastard though.

The competition took enough energy and brainpower to sober us up slightly, just enough to realize that it was now the middle of the afternoon but still early enough to take a break from the drinking get ready for the upcoming night.

Chapter 4: Johnny is Not Spiderman

One of the great ways to warm up for a night out was to tell the absurdly funny stories of the adventures of J Mac.

One that was particularly fun to tell involved his old apartment at 803 Washington Ave. (Yes, there was a life in Hoboken before 412 Monroe.) and Johnny's old roommate, a twenty something, attractive Jewish girl from Fair Lawn, NJ, named Dawn. John connected with Dawn when he was looking for his first apartment in Hoboken, but the first strike in compatibility as roommates was the fact that Dawn was also an only child.

Dawn had a bit of an uneven personality but was generally tolerant of our high level partying, while she, of course, kept one eye on any potential prospects to hook up with.

The night began innocently enough. Jude and I invited our friend Ken Wetzel, who we both knew from our time working at Macy's. Ken was a thin but conditioned guy and a former high school football player at Hillsborough High School, a wide receiver, who's claim to fame was playing football with Ricky Proehl, another wide receiver, who went on to play college football and a successful career in the NFL.

We all met at the apartment on Washington Ave. and loosened up with a few cases of beer. This place, unlike 412 Monroe, was still civilized because it was occupied by more than hard drinking mules. It was actually decorated by Dawn and therefore had a woman's influence. We all talked the usual trash talk, hung out, drank, partied, and finally, after someone noticed that it was almost 11:00 pm, we agreed on a bar and went out to hit the town.

Later that evening, after a few hours of drinking and trying to talk up some local girls, I decided to call it a night and head back.

Since it was after 1:00 am and I was hungry as usual I decided to get a slice of pizza, a typical late night routine and a great way to get some solid food in you. This being Hoboken on a Friday night there were many excellent pizza shops to choose from and every one of them was the highest quality because they were run by old school Italians. The pizza shops were most likely mob connected and fronts for a variety of miscellaneous and illegal money making activities. Though, in northern New Jersey and across the river from Manhattan, that fact was just an aside.

On a hunch that Johnny might already be home I walked past the pizza shop and continued up Washington Ave. to practically run right into a revved up and determined looking J Mac who was standing on the corner of Washington Ave. and

Eighth Ave, which exposed the back of his apartment. Johnny was looking up and staring at his building, specifically the back of his building.

It turns out that Johnny had left his keys in the apartment (again) and knew Dawn would be tough to wake up since she spent the day at *The Hunt*, a yearly fundraising event held at the fairgrounds in Far Hills, NJ. In his current state, Johnny decided that the fire escape was the perfect solution to his predicament as it was outside his bedroom window which he was sure was unlocked.

The backyard scene was right out of Brooklyn or Queens and the back of the tall brownstone apartments provided the location for every building owner to comply with the fire code by installing fire escapes. The stairs of the sturdy, welded steel fire escapes zigzagged up the building's five flights and at each floor they opened to a safe but fairly small deck. In Johnny's mind it wasn't just a deck, it was a perfect way to break into his apartment without waking his occasionally high-strung roommate.

"Johnny, what the hell are you doing here?" I asked staring and searching for the mysterious reason for Johnny's behavior.

"Dude, I'm locked out of the apartment and my roommate will freak if I knock on the door this late." Johnny answered.

No problem I thought. Let's just knock on the door. Dawn will understand, because by now she should be used to our erratic and uncivilized behavior.

Johnny had other plans. It made perfect sense (it always did).

First, he would quickly climb up a ten-foot wrought iron fence, then tightrope his way onto the roof of the garage, which was located four or five feet from the rear of the brownstone. The wrought iron fence between the brownstone and the garage would normally have made for a difficult obstacle but using his cat like agility and strength (in his mind) he intended to stealthily climb onto the top of the garage and then softly jump onto the third-floor fire escape landing. If Johnny made the jump successfully, he could quickly and easily slip in through the window then slip down and quietly open the front door for the rest of our crew.

It might have been an easy task for Spiderman or any ten-year-old boy but not so easy for a drunken, almost thirty year old guy at well past one in the morning.

Typically, I'm big on loyalty, on staying with your wing man through the battle or the attempt to talk to a hot girl in a bar, or presently the attempt by Johnny to channel Spiderman and climb up three flights using only his cat like agility and strength. But, this time something inside told me to just walk away. I told Johnny that I would see him later and walked back to the pizza shop.

I imagine there is a fine line between deserting a friend and preserving your own hide. If I was back in the Marine Corps and truly needed, I would have stuck it out. But I was not, and I couldn't talk Johnny out of his potentially disastrous plan regardless, and a couple of slices of great tasting pizza would really hit the spot right about now.

I strolled the two blocks back down Washington Ave. and into the pizza shop to discover that Jude and Ken were already there.

Great, I thought, some like minded friends to hang out with while I grab a couple of slices. Ken noticed a peculiar look on my face while I stood in line waiting to order my slices.

"Steve, what's up? You look like you saw a ghost." Ken asked with his usual sincerity.

"Well, J Mac is locked out and wants to climb up the fire escape behind the building and break into the apartment through his bedroom window." I relayed the scene to Ken and Jude, while I ordered my slices.

"Yea, two cheese slices, thanks." I shot to the shady looking Italian guy behind the counter.

"Dude why are you here getting pizza?" Jude asked, curious as usual about my excessive late night (or any time of the day) eating habits and why I wasn't back with Johnny.

I told Jude and Ken the tale of running into J Mac on the corner and his attempt to break into his own bedroom window via a wrought iron fence, a garage and the building fire escape. And as I told the story, I became more convinced of the wisdom of my decision to leave.

After my slices though, the nagging feeling that I had, in fact, abandoned my friend started to win out. The three of us left the pizza shop and walked out into the night to face whatever happened. How bad could it be? At least we wouldn't have to drive home.

As Jude, Ken and I made our way back to the apartment, screaming Hoboken police cars shot past us heading up Washington St. and as they arrived, stopping in front of 803 Washington, we quickly became curious. Just as we arrived at the doorstep, at least three or four of Hoboken's Finest ran up the stairs and into John & Dawn's apartment. The second surprise of the night occurred when just as the police disappeared into the building, Johnny emerged from the opened the apartment door for the police.

Since this was Friday night in Hoboken, the street wise police immediately began interrogating Johnny to find the gaping holes in his developing story. As Johnny explained that he actually lived in the fourth-floor apartment, the police reported that someone had just tried to break into one of the apartments via the fire escape. The plan by Hoboken's Finest to press the cross examination began to pay off and after Johnny answered all their questions the police told him to wait on the street corner while the remaining officers searched for the *burglar.*

Johnny finally walked over to Jude, Ken and I, smiled and whispered that he had a great story for us after the Hoboken Police left. As several officers emerged from the building, one of the older Sergeants approached Johnny and sternly asked,

"Was that you, who climbed in the fire escape?"

Apparently, the police had been told that a burglar had tried opening a window on the *third floor* only to find it securely locked. The third floor tenant had opened the curtains to find a tall, dark haired, twenty something, young man trying to open her window. When the *burglar* saw her, Johnny quickly climbed up to the *fourth floor* and jumped in the window, which of course per the original plan, was still open. To compound the tragic series of events, and unknown to Johnny, the police had entered the apartment via the fourth floor fire escape to search their apartment, only to discover a scared and very angry Dawn, who was awoken and seriously startled by a police flashlight shining on her face.

Eventually, after the police investigation and wrap up, Jude, Ken and I made our way back to a strange, but altogether predictable scene inside their apartment. Johnny was attempting to explain to his visibly upset (read really mad) roommate, Dawn, the reason why he decided to climb up the wrought iron fence, the garage and the building fire escape into his bedroom window at almost 2:00 in the morning.

Well, Dawn had a belly full of Johnny's crazy antics and despite his Irish charm and his great chin there was no talking his young ass out of this mess. In the end Jude and Ken and I wound up grabbing our bags and driving back home, which was more than an hour south on the Turnpike, at now closer to 3:00 in the morning. It was a tough ending to the night and another toll paid to the imaginary bridge tender for the right to hang out in Hoboken, but it was another great story to tell.

Chapter 5: The City with a Heart

Saturday night was in many ways better than Friday because, as the visiting members of the crew, we had a chance to become more acclimated to the Hoboken culture and the local scene.

For a little while the preferred lunch stop was Vito's, arguably the best sub shop in town, where you needed to have your shit together before you ordered. If you wanted the award winning fresh mozzarella on your sub you just asked for the fresh *mutz* for short. You needed to get in line, order fast and get the hell out of the way. This was the original soup Nazi, though across the Hudson and in northern Hoboken. It was just the right distance for a walk and a good excuse to get out of the apartment for a while. Another great stop for outstanding subs was Lisa's, but for now Vito's won out.

The day was cold and crisp, and it was a perfect time for a long walk north along Washington Avenue, the wide and straight artery that bisected Hoboken while running North and South. Washington Avenue ran from the Path Station and Jersey City to the South, to beyond Vito's and Weehawken to the North. To the East were the hilly and more expensive sections of Hoboken; and

Stevens Institute of Technology, then eventually the Hudson River and finally Manhattan. To the West was Willow Avenue which ran parallel to Washington, and after about ten blocks was Monroe Street and the apartment.

Between Washington Avenue and Monroe Street were hundreds of wonderful old brownstones that were once forgotten and now lay in waiting. The buildings were owned by the shrewd, old Italian birds who bought the formerly grand old homes for a song back in the 60s and 70s. These old landlords now wanted to cash in and rent out the apartments for at least two thousand dollars a month, then a princely sum. The old timers knew that Hoboken was a strategic weigh station for the upwardly mobile professionals who commanded six figures on Wall Street, they knew what the market would bear, and they were going to get every dollar they deserved.

Mixed in with the brownstones in the Spanish neighborhoods were a few wonderful bodegas. Along the southern end of Washington Ave. there was a fantastic collection of pubs, bars and restaurants. Some were small, intimate and smoky while others were large, noisy and crowded, but still smoky.

After buying our subs at Vito's, which was our one chance to have something relatively nutritious, we walked in a loose formation south along

Washington Avenue waiting to make a random right turn to head west back to the apartment.

After some trial and error and guidance from the permanent residents we found a park which was a wonderful place to throw a football around. We hung out at the park long enough to eat our subs, throw the football around and sober up a little. The apartment and all that it represented was only a few blocks away.

Monroe Street was comfortably in the Presidents section and nearly into the tougher Spanish neighborhood that was the trap for the drunken idiots who walked too far west. This would usually occur early in the morning during the dark lonely hours after a particularly rough bender and when the streets were almost empty. Thus leaving the solitary, drunken white guy vulnerable and without the safety of the numbers that protected the roaming squads.

It almost happened to me. In my case, I had tied one on well and decided to leave early, or did I start home too late? The memory of the specifics is both incomplete and hazy.

I walked home heading west past block after block of brownstones and in my haze, I kept walking past the obvious visual cues (including the fully functioning street sign with "Monroe Street" on it), which ordinarily would tell me that I needed to turn right onto Monroe Street. This time I kept walking past Monroe until I started to feel uneasy and noticed a group of younger Latino guys hanging out on the street in their world and in their terms.

I caught the eye of a large, younger looking guy still in his teens and not too cynical or aggressive yet. He noticed my stumbling and quickly realized what happened, probably thinking: *Here we go, another drunken white guy getting lost,* and he yelled over to me.

“Where do you live?” he asked

“On Monroe Street,” I replied with the best tough guy attitude I could produce, while slurring my words as I walked over to him.

“You passed it man, you better turn around and go home.” He said to me while smiling.

“Thanks man.” I smiled and mustered as hip a handshake as possible while thanking him.

The combination of his youth and my friendly reaction led to that encounter turning out great. My young, Latino friend was able to get a laugh out of my late-night stumble and I got to make it back to the apartment without being jumped.

Chapter 6: Crime and Punishment

Sometimes the walk from one bar to another was the entertainment and the highlight.

It began simply enough, when you have to go, you have to go. Mercury astronaut Alan Shepard famously urinated in his high tech (for the early Sixties) space suit. He had his reasons. His historic fifteen-minute suborbital flight was delayed for more than four hours due to the weather and last-minute preflight checks, and so after requesting and receiving permission from Mission Control, he let it rip.

We had similar reasons based on the calculus of hundreds of customers who have been drinking for hours, and the inadequacy of the rest room facilities in a typical Hoboken bar.

I'm sure it was a sight to see, a line of ten dumb, swaying and drunken white guys facing the alley wall all going at once. It was about as tactical as a Marine standing up and stretching in the middle of a firefight.

"Get in line you assholes!" The shouting started so suddenly that we all thought it was a joke.

The local cops were dammed mad. First, they were mad at the fact that we were obnoxious enough to think we could get away with our brazen act of defiance, when in fact we were just drunk and dumb. Second, they were mad that they had to work on a Saturday night, while we were out partying and having a great time. And finally, they were mad at us for basically ignoring them initially, when, in reality, we were just too drunk to react quicker.

So, these local boys in blue decide to really lay it on thick and march (yes, march) the whole assortment of us dumb drunks in a squad formation (for the uninitiated that means in a single file line) all the way across Washington Ave. to Hoboken City Hall, while shouting at us like boot camp drill instructors to keep our mouths shut.

Had I not managed to survive real boot camp I might have been a little scared, but it all seemed pretty funny at the time. For our part, the lot of us really didn't seem to appreciate the gravity of this incident. It was either that, or the amount of drinking we had already done had successfully obliterated any feelings of embarrassment or even awareness. In short, we were just too drunk to really care.

This seemed to ramp up the excitement level of our local boys in blue. So, off we went marching (yes, marching) under orders from Hoboken's finest, in full display of the prime-time Saturday night Hoboken crowd, right up the stairs of City Hall and into the main entrance of Hoboken Police Headquarters. The balance of the night involved getting ticketed with a misdemeanor charge of urinating in public, not exactly a resume builder, but neither was it a felony.

It was the price you had to pay every now and then, the toll you had to hand over to the imaginary bridge tender for hanging out in Hoboken, our version of Sin City.

A few weeks later, the court summons arrived to tell us of the chance to appear with all the other dumb drunks, bad drivers and various other sub felonious offenders.

I already knew the drill from my many previous court appearances during my years of substandard driving. The many red lights and stop signs and speed limits that I mange to ignore while living and pretending to care about driving in the Garden State.

I was the character in Springsteen's, *State Trooper,* who pleads not to be stopped and considers his fate:

New Jersey Turnpike riding on a wet night

'Neath the refinery's glow out where the great black rivers flow

License, registration, I ain't got none

But I got a clear conscience 'bout the things that I done

Mister state trooper, please don't stop me

Please don't stop me, please don't stop me")

Having been there many times before, I patiently sat in the packed courtroom and waited for my name to be called. When the time came I stood up and walked in front of the judge and pleaded dumb (the official term is "guilty"). The judge, numb from the hundreds, probably thousands, of equally dumb, though not exactly hardened, sub felonious criminals that he had sentenced in his many years on the bench, announced my verdict: Two hundred and fifty dollars fine and eight hours of community service.

I must admit it stung, and the amount of the fine was an especially bitter pill to swallow. After six years of college and my entry level salary, I wasn't exactly solvent. But let's look on the bright side, if I paid the fine and did the community service it was like it never happened. Let's call it what it

really was: a slap on the wrist. Still, I left the courthouse and headed home feeling defeated.

The very next weekend I drove up to 412 Monroe to for a repeat performance of the high-level partying and we all began to commiserate on our court appearances and sentencing for our lack of bladder control and general drunken thoughtlessness the week before.

As expected, we all got the same slap on the wrist: Two hundred and fifty dollar fine and one day of community service. OK, that sounds about right. But the ridiculous bit of good luck that followed made the experience turn out just fine in the end. After a couple of weeks and all of us comparing notes it became apparent that we all had the same day of community service (for some strange reason, all of us except Danny, who scored a different day).

The same dim light bulb flickered on in all our clouded heads. Let's meet at the apartment and get lit up before the community service, why not?

The big day finally arrives, and eight o' clock on a Saturday morning sort of hurt us. But the whole gang was together, J Mac, Jimmy, Jude, Odie and me, along with a few other local characters. How bad could it be? We left the apartment feeling no pain and head to a nondescript municipal garage that could have easily served as a set for any prime time, network crime drama.

The weather had been threatening all morning, and by the time we begin our service of picking up any, and all trash that we find in the street, a light rain begins to fall. The city municipal worker who was stuck with the job of supervising us on this Saturday morning started out less than enthusiastic, and by the time it starts to rain he is looking downright dejected.

Then the joking around begins to pick up steam. Odie gets the ball rolling by picking up a dead bird, a big one too, with his government issued shovel and asks our less than faithful supervisor.

"Is this considered trash?" After that a slight smile began to form on our Hoboken born and bred, long haired and professionally limited supervisor.

We all laugh at Odie's joke and start to notice that the rain is really coming down heavy now. This was the last straw for our not so faithful supervisor. He looks at us, looks at his watch, by now it was almost 10:30 am, and he looks back at us. It was only two and a half hours into our eight hours of community service, and he announces to us that we are done.

We have fulfilled our community service commitment and we are all free to go. Thank you, God, for the perfect combination of a well timed rainstorm and an exceptionally lazy municipal worker! Back to the apartment we go, back to a decent breakfast a little partying and some more Rho Sham Bo. We all celebrated our blind, dumb luck and relaxed the morning away.

Chapter 7: Mardi Gras?

It was now late Saturday afternoon; the day was wearing on and dusk was turning to night. The stories were still being told and another "Ro-Sham-Bo" competition was initiated to determine who would get stuck buying the next case of beer.

The universe had conspired to supply us with a cozy, family owned convenience store a couple of houses down on Monroe St. and even in our perpetually hazy state this good fortune did not go unnoticed. With a solid supply of beer to take us past the showering and prepping portion of the day the energy levels ticked up a couple of notches.

The railroad setup of the apartment didn't help the cause of getting the six or seven drunken and dirty mules relatively well dressed and presentable. Jimmy typically took the brunt of the confused and wandering masses that needed to cross through his bedroom that bordered the combination den and living room.

While we showered and dressed we drank and plotted and used the brutal honesty of our good friends to hone our skills and methods for attracting the many girls that would be out on a Saturday night.

Jude would typically bring a few well coordinated outfits and after a brief hiatus from the fun of the den, he would reappear dressed in something out of a Ralf Lauren catalog and wait for the response. The inevitable reaction was both swift and brutal. Jude would usually go back and try out another outfit which was equally well coordinated, and eventually equilibrium was established which balanced the determination of Jude to dress well and the alcohol fueled criticism of everyone else in the apartment.

"Jude, that shirt is totally gay." Johnny fired the first shot across the bow.

"Dude, the last time I saw that outfit was in the gay pride parade," snapped Jimmy, who saw a good opportunity for a one-two punch.

"I thought I saw Jude in the parade last year." Odie connected nicely with a well-timed zinger.

"Fuck you guys, chicks dig me." Jude held his ground, though he did have a point. Jude had the good fortune to be the youngest of seven in a traditional Irish family of mostly sisters who successfully taught him the ways of the female gender. Jude's confidence was his main tool of the trade and he knew he would do well, while the girl he set his sights on typically appreciated his efforts. If he wasn't too far gone, then the scene could get a bit ugly.

During one of the relatively sober moments in the apartment a great idea sprang out of a normal afternoon of partying and trash talking in 412 Monroe.

"We should do Mardi Gras in New Orleans this year," someone announced. (Again, it made perfect sense.) Why not take our game up a notch? Why not gather all eight or nine of us down in the original party city, the authentic center of the drinking man's universe?

The hotel was found and the flights were booked, the weeks of anticipation were reduced to a few days and finally we were all on our flights down to New Orleans.

For me, the sign of good times to come appeared in the form of a sidewalk beer cart as soon as I stepped out of my old, broken down cab that I caught at the airport. The beer cart was a fine idea that was a strange and inviting sight. It was however a perfectly normal accessory for the Crescent City.

My decision making was rather easy: I saw a beer cart and then I bought a beer. While doing this I disregarded many relatively important facts which included: My time in New Orleans proper was less than five minutes; I was still carrying around my luggage; and I still needed to find the hotel. But I could do all those things and still have a beer in the process, couldn't I? The comfort of the sound logic of the near alcoholic was like a warm blanket.

I walked up Canal Street towards the Mississippi river while noticing that the French Quarter was alive with fellow partiers from across America and I quickly realized that I was just another tourist. Our hotel, the Le Madeleine, was on Canal Street a few blocks from the top of Bourbon Street. I strolled into the French themed lobby and coaxed the hotel room number for the McCauley's' from the hotel registration staff. After a few minutes in the elevator, I had finally made to our southern hub for Mardi Gras.

The long weekend in New Orleans was a notch or two higher than the Hoboken scene, because it was Bourbon Street in the French Quarter and we had arrived in the drinking man's heaven. We roamed around drinking beer and Hurricanes from the street vendors and after unknown hours we eventually decided to stop wandering around and find a good bar.

Since we were all tourists, we settled on Pat O'Brien's bar for a little while. We drank and partied and met the locals and Southerners, including one older gentleman we called "Jimmy". As long as the booze was flowing (and on our tab) *Jimmy* stuck close to our little group. We drank at the bar and tried to have a few decent conversations with the locals.

When we finally became restless again we left the bar and roamed around some more while we asked the drunken and willing, young girls to lift their shirts in exchange for a few beads.

After an unknown period of time and to everyone's delight and satisfaction Danny decided to set up shop in one of the gentlemen's clubs. This was an especially great deal for us because we all had an especially high level of appreciation for a good gentlemen's club, and the clubs were all revved up for Mardi Gras. We stayed at the club for a little while and had our fun.

After a couple of hours in this perfectly legal and acceptable den of sin we left to hit Bourbon Street for a street side vendor to buy another beer, wander through the masses and stumble into the next bar. The theme for this trip was endurance drinking and for this competition we were all highly trained athletes.

At some unknown point I wandered away from the group and was walking on a street parallel to Bourbon Street when I noticed a collection of large guys walking in a pack that I guessed to be the rest of the crew. When I saw them, all formed up in a circle attempting to start a round of Rho Sham Bo, I knew it was them. I ran up to the circle and jumped in with my *rock* while loudly announcing that I was in. Of course, everyone else somehow managed to throw a *paper* while I threw a *rock*.

Goddamn wonderful luck, I lost on the first round with almost ten players. Naturally I broke out my wallet and bought the nine or ten beers to satisfy the unwritten laws of Rho Sham Bo.

One of the early, spring thunderstorms that slowly passed across New Orleans gave us a strong hint to give the hard corps partying a break while we all made our way back to the hotel. As the steady rain washed the spilled drinks and other numerous by-products of the excessive partying from the dirty, city streets, we hung out and rested in the hotel room. The drinking continued but the pace slowed slightly while we trash talked and alternated between watching ESPN and the dark, storm clouds and lightning from twenty stories up.

During a break in the action Johnny, Danny, Odie were sitting near the window with a friend of Odie's named Ray. Ray was recruited to make the trip by Odie and was a good addition. (Loosely translated that meant that he contributed to paying for the hotel room and beers and didn't annoy anyone.) Ray found himself in the spotlight for a while because of his weight. He had a jump start on the middle age bulge and this fact didn't go unnoticed by Johnny.

"Dude, you're not thin," Johnny zinged Ray while almost insisting that Ray agree with him.

"Come on I'm not fat though," Ray tried in vain to defend himself from the attack.

“Honestly dude, you're definitely not thin,” Johnny was unrelenting.

Ray's friends laughed at him and even started agreeing with Johnny while the loyalty quickly began to fade. The whole time Johnny was zinging Ray I was standing nearby hanging out.

“A bunch of rats jumping off a sinking ship,” I couldn't resist chiming in. Odie was the only one who heard me and laughed.

“Fuck the cheese, let's get the hell out of here,” I continued finally getting a decent laugh from the balance of the guys.

We hung out in the hotel room and when the storm cleared we ventured out of the hotel and into the great partying unknown again.

The trip lasted four days and nights while we drank from morning to night and succeeded in taking our home game down to New Orleans and Mardi Gras. Some highlights included: Waiting on the curb at the entrance of the bar at 9:00 am, getting drunk at Pat O’Brien’s and renting a *Jimmy*, and finally ending with the quote: “Stop the ride I want to get off.” We caught the flights home and tried our best to resume our lives.

Chapter 8: Just be Yourself

Once we fully recovered from New Orleans we resumed our weekends in Hoboken, at the apartment on 412 Monroe Street.

It was finally almost 10:00 pm on Saturday night and we were revved up for a great night of drinking and trash talking. We had all done our best to get ready for a night of competition.

To refine our *rap,* we would try it out on the present company and in the confines of the apartment where everyone would try their best to support the cause. We were all single though and we all wanted essentially the same thing. Once we were out in a good bar looking for the opportunity to put all the training and refining into practice, the competitive instincts kicked in and the friendly rivalry back at 412 Monroe evolved into a jump ball.

Out in a good bar anyone who had the quickness and intellectual agility would be the first one to gain the possession. The game would continue all night though and every game has its share of turnovers.

After a solid amount of partying was accomplished at 412 Monroe, and after someone noticed that it was almost 11:00 pm, we finally hit the streets and walked up to Washington Ave.

Keeping with the routine of a typical Saturday night the first stop was one of the solid Irish pubs along Washington Ave. The rounds of pints began with ten or twelve thick glasses of beers at a time. We drank the pints while we fueled our good times and kept the spirits high. We hung out and warmed up while we trash talked with each other and talked up some of the girls in the pub.

Eventually we agreed to move to Texas Arizona where it was crowded, smoky and loud, and absolutely a hit. After a little while we noticed a group of girls who seemed too nice for the typical Jersey scene and too friendly for the local Hoboken crowd (the over worked commuters on the Path trains who were one step away from working and living in Manhattan, and who would hit the bars on the way home to blow off some steam). This group of girls seemed friendly enough to be approachable. Since the crowd was stronger and denser than usual we took a few minutes to search around for a good place to hang out.

During this initial break in the action while I was still fairly revved up and feeling no pain, I quietly noticed a pretty blonde alone in the crowd. While Eddie Vetter sang his song of redemption to encourage me, I decided to storm the beach, to walk over alone and vulnerable. I elbowed my way into the crowd and walked over to where she was standing, simultaneously blocking the flow of people and creating some space for us to talk. My opening line was a simple introduction. When I learned what her name was, next came:

"Where are you from?"

"California," she answered, while I smiled and celebrated my luck. I knew all about Southern California from being stationed at Camp Pendleton, which was on the Pacific coast between San Diego and Los Angeles.

"Really, I was stationed out there..."

The conversation went on effortlessly and long enough for all of her friends to join her. I was suddenly in a great place. I was among a group of friendly and attractive girls, talking to one of their friends who seemed to sincerely enjoy my company. This fact did not go unnoticed by the boys and the rest of the troops elbowed their way into the crowd to make the walk over to join me. Jude and Johnny, the St. Joseph contingent, along with Odie and Jimmy, had arrived to make inroads with their own introductions and smoothly kept the conversations going while the pints kept flowing.

We found out soon that the girls were newly hired flight attendants working for Continental Airlines. (Johnny would later meet and hit it off with one, a pretty brunette named Paula.)

For most of the night Johnny just kept talking, it's what he did best. His conversations would start and stop and begin again, and meander in and out of the grey area between fact and fiction and back to non-fiction. All the while the reassuring sound of his voice was there, filling the void and keeping the momentum going, while entertaining everyone within earshot. Odie and Jimmy hung out and talked up the girls while Jimmy kept the jokes and laughs going.

This night was the classic case of preparation meeting opportunity. We were all happily drunk and buzzed and out for a great time in a fun town that was full of bars, which were full of groups of similarly intoxicated and single, young girls. It was obvious that these flight attendants were out looking for a good time. What great luck, and what a great opportunity to put into action the plotting and planning and the confidence building trash talking back at the apartment.

We talked to these pretty, young girls and drank the pints and made good fun of each other while we jousted and tested the boundaries. We did this and had the time of our lives, because we could, and because we all knew that we had found our niche.

"Dude, I have a great dimples," Johnny said to no one while there was a break in the conversation with the flight attendants. He was so proud of his goddamn dimples. Johnny considered it to be his genetic edge, his one step advantage that allowed the predator to outrun and catch his prey.

We all searched and maneuvered for that edge, the crack in the armor and the means that allowed us to achieve that wonderful moment when the girl you were trying to impress was fairly impressed with you, the rare time when you could stop posturing and be yourself. When that happened, you could finally enjoy the moment and each other, while the music and the crazy, crowded scene at the bar gave you the background and the set.

We talked and drank some more and finally when it was almost closing time, and after the phone numbers had been exchanged, we all left the bar. On the way home, the guys who did well made sure everyone knew about it.

The next morning came swift and early and the bodies littered the apartment. The apartment was by now, Sunday morning and nearly the end of the amusement park ride of a weekend, absolutely trashed. The movements began slowly but the jokes were swift and spontaneous while the old habits surfaced.

"Jimmy! Where the hell is my wallet!?"

www.ingramcontent.com/pod-product-compliance
Ingram Content Group UK Ltd.
Pitfield, Milton Keynes, MK11 3LW, UK
UKHW041836200726
13854UKWH00003BA/1160

9 781304 043535